Dalziel + Scullion

#

The Fruitmarket Gallery
Edinburgh, 2001

There is an anaesthetic of familiarity, a sedative of ordinariness, which dulls the senses and hides the wonder of existence. But we can recapture that sense of having just entered in on life, of having been newly placed on the earth, by looking at our world in unfamiliar ways.

Richard Dawkins, *Unweaving the Rainbow*

Contents

Dalziel + Scullion by Keith Hartley

We are living at a critical juncture in the relationship between humanity and Nature. Intense economic competition on a global scale, coupled with population growth and rapid scientific developments, have put unprecedented pressure on the natural environment and led to repeated crises. In our own corner of north west Europe alone we have witnessed the depletion of fish stocks in the North Sea, the BSE epidemic and, most recently, the lightning spread of foot and mouth disease. We can no longer be so optimistic about our ability to master Nature and bend it to our will, at least not without its biting back in an unpredictable and often nasty manner. The days of an unquestioning and naïve optimism in the march of human progress now seem past.

We look back with nostalgia and envy at past generations who believed in scientific and social utopias, and who set out enthusiastically to help bring them about. Much of the Modern Movement in art and architecture was predicated on this unshakeable faith in the human ability to create a future built upon rational principles. Accordingly, no longer would the vagaries of external Nature be allowed to stand in the way of pure reason. Nature's secret principles would be laid bare and used to construct a new, artificial world. In Russia, after the Revolution, the Constructivists and Supremacists made visionary blueprints for the future in the form of abstract paintings and sculptures. Architects rejected past traditions, and embraced instead new social needs and new industrial materials and techniques. Unlike classical or medieval architecture, their buildings stood against nature rather than growing out of it. In Germany, the Bauhaus

designers sought to begin afresh from first principles. Their buildings and design products have come to epitomise for us the Modern Movement. Clean, uncluttered lines, simple shapes, no ornamentation, a rational analysis of the needs of the user and of how best to fulfil them: in a word, functional. Some artists eulogised this brave new world. Fernand Léger's paintings of the 1920s are a hymn to a completely artificial, man-made environment with the city and the machine as its supreme achievements.

This Modernist dream and the heroic attempt to turn that dream into reality act as both leitmotif and touchstone in the work of Dalziel and Scullion. Frequently they use Modernist forms and structures in their art: the perfect circle in *The Gifted Child* (1995), the rectangular box in *Sargassum* (1995), the simplified windows and ramp in *Endlessly* (1996/97), the elegant curves of *The Horn* (1997), the cubic pavilion of *Rain* (2000) and the artificial, circular stone nests of the penguins in *Habitat* (2001). Dalziel and Scullion are drawn to Modernism by the formal clarity of its structures, by its fresh optimism and by its lack of sentimentality. But they are deeply aware that it is nevertheless flawed, because it fails to take the extent of Nature's power and complexities fully into account. In this they join company with one of the key figures in the critique of Modernism, Robert Smithson. The Modernism that Smithson took issue with was more specific to the visual arts and had been given programmatic formulation in post-war America by critics such as Clement Greenberg and Michael Fried. The latter argued that the inner logic of each art form was to reduce itself to those aspects central to its specific nature. In a celebrated formulation of this doctrine Greenberg wrote in 1961:

'It quickly emerged that the unique and proper area of competence of each art coincided with all that was unique to the nature of its medium. The task of self-criticism became to eliminate from the effects of each art any and every effect that might conceivably be borrowed from or by the medium of any other art. Thereby each art would be rendered 'pure', and in its 'purity' find the guarantee of its standards of quality as well as of its independence.'[1]

Smithson objected to the whole notion of purity in art, because it cut art off from life's experiences; it isolated art from its wider context. In an interview given in 1972 he expressed his objections succinctly: 'Art has tended to be viewed in terms of isolation, neutralisation, separation, and this is encouraged. Art is supposed to be on some eternal plane, free from the experiences of the world, and I'm more interested in these experiences, not as a refutation of art, but as art as part of that experience, or interwoven, in other words, all these factors come into it.'[2] Smithson, through his writings as well as his art, helped usher in an art that was equally interested in content and form, that considered as paramount the context(s) in which art was made and shown, and that constantly referred to the wider world of Nature. Associated initially with Minimalism, Smithson was one of the main practitioners of Land Art and one of the founding fathers of modern-day Environmental Art. His writings about art, Nature and society are so full of startling insight and fresh thinking that they still inspire artists today.

Dalziel and Scullion are no exceptions. Scullion studied Environmental Art at Glasgow School of Art at a crucial period in the mid to late 1980s. The department had recently been set up under David Harding and had a group of students all eager to move away from the current trend in expressionist, figurative painting.[3] The obvious models internationally were those artists in the late 1960s who rebelled against the current Modernist orthodoxies in painting and sculpture. Prime among them were Smithson and Dan Graham. In Scotland there was an earlier generation of artists such as Glen Onwin, Eileen Lawrence, Elizabeth Ogilvie and Robert Callander (mainly based in Edinburgh), who had themselves been inspired by Smithson and his environmental approach to art. Ian Hamilton Finlay was also a key figure on several levels. Not only did he work directly in and with the landscape, but he moved easily between media (carving, casting, neon, photography, sound, text).

From 1987-88 Dalziel studied sculpture and photography at Glasgow. The two artists began collaborating in 1993. The first work they made together, *The Bathers* (1993), gives some indication of the direction in which their work would go. It consists of three glass cubicles, through which one can see the projection of three videos. These show three individuals (one a swimmer) in their own specific environments. The cubicles have slatted wooden floors and benches such as one would find in changing rooms; the use of glass for the wall, even if frosted, works against but does not wholly negate this perception. The general feeling of the structures is one of Scandinavian Modernism; of light, sun, naturism and healthy outdoor pursuits. The projected images reinforce this impression. With *The Bathers* Dalziel and Scullion established some of the basic parameters and common features of their work: the mixture of video and Modernist structures, and the recording of individuals in their own environment. Dan Graham had also created glazed pavilions in which visitors could view videos since 1986, but his intentions had been quite different. There, the pavilions were at once functional exhibition structures and places in which to watch other people's reactions to the videos and to each other. They were social spaces.

The cubicles in *The Bathers* are not so much concerned with social interaction as with functioning on an associational level. The viewer has to enter each cubicle to see the videos thus putting him or herself into the place of a potential bather, of someone in intimate contact with Nature.

Two years later, in 1995, Dalziel and Scullion worked with Visual Art Projects in Glasgow on a project that developed several of the themes in *The Bathers* and brought them to a new coherence. *The Gifted Child* consisted of a large sheet of glass suspended from a tree in Rouken Glen Park.[4] A circle, 4 feet in diameter, was sandblasted in the centre of the glass, and onto this Dalziel and Scullion projected alternate footage of the surface of the North Sea and of a swimmer practising synchronised movements. In effect the artists set up two

parallel juxtapositions: the first, between the organic, natural setting (albeit tamed, since it was a park) and the geometrically shaped sheet of glass, a man-made product; the second, between the natural, rhythmic movements of the sea and the tightly-controlled and choreographed movements of the swimmer. The artists make no overt comment about the relationship between humans and their natural environment, although the extreme artificiality of the swimmer's movements (Dalziel and Scullion have called synchronised swimming 'the bonsai of the water world') give us pause for thought as to how we humans use our natural environment: fighting against it and exploiting it rather than working with it. At this stage in their career the artists had moved to the north east coast of Scotland, and were only too aware of the exploitation of the North Sea's natural resources.

The sea and our relationship with it is the subject of their next major project. *Sargassum* was made for an exhibition of young British artists organised by the British Council to coincide with the Venice Biennale in 1995.[5] This time Dalziel and Scullion did not use video, but relied instead on light and movement. The work consisted of two parallel walls some 11 feet apart. A semi-transparent cloth was stretched over the gap between the walls, covering the ends of the structure. Fifty blue electric light-bulbs were placed on the floor between the walls, each fitted with an aluminium disc that rotated as the heat rose from the bulb. The resulting pulses of light and heat caused the sheet at the top to glow and ripple rhythmically. The effect on the viewer was mesmeric, inducing a hypnotic state. As the title suggests, the work evoked the slow-moving, becalmed waters of the Sargasso Sea, but also, in view of the location, the trapped waters of the Venetian lagoon. There is a deliberate disproportion between the small, restricted, geometric structure with its (clearly visible) low-tech apparatus, and the awesome vastness and complicated ecology of the Sargasso Sea. And yet this simple creation is able to evoke that very vastness, and to draw forth our wonder at the unfathomable mysteries of Nature. As Dalziel and Scullion have explained: 'All the evidence of how *Sargassum* worked, how it originated, was present and yet the thing still retained a mystery. I think that is the essence of what we are aiming for in our work. What we are trying to do is to explore mystery and wonder. Not to explain them away – people need mystery and faith in mystery – but just to show that often this originates from within human beings.'

When Dalziel and Scullion moved to St Combs in the north east of Scotland they were confronted by very real juxtapositions of human technological structures and the natural world. This is a relatively remote, largely agricultural part of Scotland, and yet it contains some of Europe's most sophisticated industrial installations – a huge gas production plant and Ministry of Defence communications systems. Wild fowl sanctuaries sit next to high-tech equipment. Just as a hide and wooden walkway through the marshes allow visitors to view the birds unseen, so the aerials and satellite dishes allow land-based monitors to keep track of distant ships and aircraft. The two co-exist in an uneasy symbiosis, perhaps signalling the birth of a new technological Nature.

Dalziel and Scullion's next work, *Endlessly* (1996-97), also reflects this possibility. In it two large architectural structures are set opposite one another. Both resemble large windows but one has two steps leading up to it, the other a ramp. The windows are in fact screens. Onto the first the silhouetted image of an angel, a Victorian tombstone carving, is projected, showing it in the changing light conditions from morning to night. On the second we see the surface of the sea from above, the waves creating an endless rhythmic pattern. If the angel represents conventional religious belief, historically contingent, the sea represents Nature's continuous and unchanging presence. *Endlessly* is one of Dalziel and Scullion's most overtly religious works: religious in the sense that the structures suggest altars, and the images parallel (or opposing?) ways to approach death and the infinite. The work also has a soundtrack of wavelike, 'unending' music, interspersed with natural sounds such as the calling of gulls and the barking of a dog, which acts as a powerful aid to contemplation. The Modernist forms of the structure housing the video of the sea make one think of futuristic dreams of salvation in Space (the ramp to a spaceship?), but the image of the sea points to salvation closer to home.

Site-specific commissions have formed an important part of Dalziel and Scullion's work. In 1997 they completed two very different pieces: *The Horn* and *Migrator*. *The Horn*, perhaps because of its long lead-in time (it was commissioned in the early 1990s), addresses different issues to the artists' other contemporary work. Situated just off the M8 motorway, midway between Edinburgh and Glasgow, it stands like a sentinel greeting the passing motorists with its strange, shiny presence. Its elegant shape is vaguely reminiscent of structures such as foghorns or telecommunication masts, but it is plainly neither of these. It seems alien, an arrival from a future time – sent perhaps to warn us and give us advice. And yet the sounds that it broadcasts are not alien, but distinctly contemporary and recognisable. There is music, humming, speeches by well-known international figures and above all comments on land use, ecology and wildlife. The corridor between Glasgow and Edinburgh through which the motorway passes contains much evidence of human disregard for the environment, of ruthless exploitation of natural resources. The messages broadcast by *The Horn* thus take on a very real relevance to their surroundings. The work has since become a landmark for commuters who pass it every day. Its shape has impressed itself on their consciousness, and its occasionally heard broadcasts have made them wonder if they are official pronouncements. It has become familiar, and yet it remains unsettling – a nagging reminder from a future age that we are the guardians of the present and must cherish it.

Migrator, on the other hand, commissioned by BAA for its New World Business Centre at Heathrow Airport, sets up specific relationships between Nature and modern technology. The high-tech building is situated between a busy road feeding cars relentlessly into the airport and the aircraft taxiways. Two television monitors sit on the ground floor playing ongoing footage of the sea; opposite, the viewer can see aircraft preparing to take to the skies or landing on the runway. Dalziel and Scullion decided that in such a spectacular setting there was no point in trying to compete visually, so they chose instead to broadcast the calls of migratory birds that frequent Britain's wetlands and moors: Canadian Greylag Geese, Great Northern Divers, Curlews, Dunlin and Bittern. Their haunting sounds make the planes and their activities look as strange and unnatural as they really are; giant mechanical birds, migrating huge distances from continent to continent in a matter of hours. The simplicity of means used by the artists to link the disparate elements makes the work effective and compelling.

In 2000, Oriel 31 commissioned Dalziel and Scullion to make a work for the grounds of their gallery in Newtown, Wales. Since the piece would be there throughout the winter the artists decided to focus on what would be one of the most prominent features of the site at that time, namely rain. They built a pavilion that could be used to experience rain in all its facets. An initial stimulus for the concept of *Rain* had come from a woodcut by Hiroshige entitled *Moon-Viewing Platform*. Since rain is one of the most pronounced features of life in Wales as well as Scotland, the artists decided to build something to celebrate and enjoy it rather than shutting it out. As with *Migrator*, the idea is very simple and all the more effective for that reason. The structure is light and airy – not high-tech, but made of simple materials (corrugated tin for the roof that amplified the sound of falling rain, lightweight plastic for the walls that refracted the light during the day and could be lit at night). It has the feeling of a Japanese pavilion; in harmony with the elements, not opposing them. At night the building was transformed from a place in which to contemplate the rain to a luminous spectacle viewed from outside. Gobos were directed onto its reflecting surfaces, creating rhythmically modulated rain patterns.

In *Rain,* Dalziel and Scullion aimed at and achieved a fine sense of harmony between humanity and the natural environment. The pavilion was not at odds with its surroundings. In another major work from 2000, *Modern Nature*, the relationship is more strained, even bleak. *Modern Nature* was carried out for the Tyrebagger Trust on Elrick Hill near Aberdeen. It looks back to *The Horn* in its use of futuristic, high-tech structures, but also to *Migrator* in its marrying of Nature and technology. The work consists of six five-metre high aluminium poles surmounted by solar panels. These provide the power for underground speakers that periodically broadcast the sound of a Capercaillie. This, one of Scotland's largest and most impressive birds, is no longer extant on Elrick Hill; indeed, the Capercaillie died out in Scotland in 1784 and had to be reintroduced from Scandinavia in 1830. Now its numbers are once more in decline. J. G. Ballard once ironically suggested that if we knew the DNA details of endangered species we could in the future resurrect them through modern technology. The mournful truth is that all we can do now is to recall memories of their presence. Dalziel and Scullion have therefore reintroduced its unmistakeable territorial call.

The area around Elrick Hill is similar to that surrounding Dalziel and Scullion's former home at St Combs. It seems to be completely rural, even wild and untouched, yet in reality it is hedged around by industrial and domestic developments. Helicopters travelling to off-shore oil platforms in the North Sea, aeroplanes landing and departing at Aberdeen airport, cell phone transmitters – all these can be seen from Elrick Hill, even though it is covered with heather and surrounded by forest. *Modern Nature* suggests that this symbiosis is here to stay.

In addition to public art projects and gallery installations, Dalziel and Scullion have made a number of films. *The Pressure of Spring,* commissioned by Channel Four Television in 1999, is about the lives of young people in the rural environment of north east Scotland. It demonstrates the connectedness with Nature that still exists in that part of the world – whether it is through work, in fish processing, or through leisure, in dune driving and surfing. As in so much of their work, though, Dalziel and Scullion show that this closeness to Nature does not exclude familiarity with worldwide technological networks. *Another Place* (2000) was also filmed in the north east, and focuses on a number of people living in the same village as the artists. Shot in close-up, with their heads set against their environment – the sea, their places of work, their homes – the subjects look totally at one with their surroundings. Confident, content, rooted. The film is slowed down so that, at first, one is not aware that the people are moving. Since the film is projected onto a wall, the figures look as if they have been captured in large-scale colour photographs, reminiscent of the work of Thomas Ruff or Rineke Dijkstra.

Since 1997, Dalziel and Scullion have been making field trips to Norway, during which they have worked mainly in an area around the Jostedalsbreen Glacier near Fjaerland. This experience changed their whole perception of Nature. In Scotland, Nature had long been altered, domesticated, hedged in – an adjunct to human settlement. In Norway much of it was still raw, wild and untouched, and the gradual melting and receding of the glacier gave an insight as to how land had been formed millions of years ago. Moving away from the foot of the glacier one could trace the series of developments that produced the countryside we know now. Just as the quarries and industrial zones of New Jersey had given Smithson an awareness of the ineluctable nature of time and entropy – to the extent that even art could not escape into a timeless present – so the glaciers of Norway gave pause to Dalziel and Scullion's belief in an inevitable synthesis between Nature and technology. Perhaps there was something sacred about wildernesses and the need to conserve what was left of them.[6] However, modern technology could be used to capture the essence of such areas and bring them into our own technologically bound lives.

A series of current works by Dalziel and Scullion concentrates on precisely this project. For the foyer areas of Sadler's Wells Theatre in London they have created *Meltwater*, a tri-partite work that has as its theme the primordial grandeur of the landscape downstream from a receding glacier. The first part of the work, *Path*, comprises a digital image of a footpath leading away into the distance where a glacier can be seen. It is printed in circular form (reminiscent of *The Gifted Child*) on a flowing curtain, thus relating it to the idea of a theatrical curtain and to the building in which the work hangs. The path may symbolise the pilgrimage that we humans increasingly feel the need to take to escape our urban environment and submit ourselves to Nature's raw power. Theatres have traditionally fulfilled this role, purifying our emotions in a cathartic climax. But the path may also be seen as leading away from the glacier, away from life's origins and down through successive bands of organic sophistication until it reaches human civilisation. *Valley*, the second part of *Meltwater*, is made up of a series of lozenge-shaped photographic images stretched over padded supports, giving them the appearance of Modernist design features. They show a scree of rocks and boulders on a mountainside with trees beginning to get a hold in their midst, preparing the way for blanket plant coverage. Lastly, *Ice Stream* is a video presentation which shows the meltwater from the glacier forming a stream, opaque with suspended granite dust that the glacier has scraped from the rocks. To our urban eyes this looks like chemical pollution, but in fact this mineral solution forms the basis of lowland fertility. The only problem is that global warming has speeded up this process and threatens the very existence of the glaciers.

Although *Meltwater* continues Dalziel and Scullion's practice of linking Nature with Modernist forms, the emphasis has switched from structures to images. These are now so powerful and overwhelming, with the absence of features like the sky to relate to, that our human scale is crushed. In a new work, *Drift*, that they are preparing for their exhibition at The Fruitmarket Gallery, they redress this balance by mounting photographic images on screens which can potentially be moved at will. Nature at its most raw and majestic seems domesticated, reduced to something that humans can manipulate to suit their pleasure. Painted screens have been a feature of Japanese art for centuries, and mountain scenery has been a popular subject to put on them. By putting photographic images on their screens, however, Dalziel and Scullion have brought Nature untransformed by artistic stylisation into the gallery space. Living as we do in a largely artificial environment, we are thus forced to question our place both in our own world and in the natural world (or what is left of it). In *Habitat*, also part of the Fruitmarket exhibition, we are invited to watch groups of penguins making themselves at home in artificial, concrete 'nests' in a Bergen Zoo. Round and beautifully fashioned, the nests look like Modernist carvings from the 1920s or 30s. As an integral part of the work, the room also contains a carpet and a group of contemporary armchairs. Whilst conjuring up a domestic space, these items of furniture also contribute to a futuristic atmosphere – one in which the idea of outside and inside, of the raw and the cultivated is questioned.

Closely connected to the 'Norwegian' works, and to the theme of wilderness, is a recent work, *Voyager*, which also appears in the Fruitmarket exhibition. Three cast aluminium tents, similar to those used in serious expeditions to the wilder corners of our planet, sit on a scree of grey ash. They look as if they belong either to a distant past, preserved intact like fossils, or to a distant future, their shiny surfaces reminiscent of B movie spaceships. In either case they look like evidence of some catastrophe that has befallen the earth. The ash suggests that the world has been reduced to a barren, burnt-out landscape. The tents suggest the human pioneering spirit, lone individuals battling against the elements. *Voyager* is Dalziel and Scullion's bleakest work, an apocalyptic vision of what might happen to the earth if humanity continues on its present course. And yet hope clings on. The tents may still contain life, just as dried-out pods contain seeds capable of germinating, should conditions improve.

Dalziel and Scullion are currently working on a public art commission that has distinctly religious overtones. *Bell*, a

project initiated by the Pier Art Centre in Orkney, will be situated high up on the cliffs at Yesnaby, reached only after a long walk. After completing this pilgrimage visitors will be invited to ring a bell hanging low down from a tall, gate-like metal framework. Just as climbers put a stone on a cairn to mark their successful ascent of a peak, or pilgrims light a candle when they arrive at the shrine of a saint, so visitors can mark their arrival by ringing the bell. The gate-like structure, framing both sky and sea, will also serve to focus the feelings of visitors, encouraging them to contemplate the elements. It will be like a threshold onto another plane.

Such an invitation to pause and consider our position in the natural order, to contemplate what is sublime in Nature, is central to Dalziel and Scullion's work. As we busy ourselves with our own small corner of the world, our own allotted role in life, so cut off do we feel from our roots, from a sense of the whole, that any glimpse of a still intact universe beyond can lift us temporarily out of our present, contingent reality. This is the impulse that lies behind most religions. It is also one of the key principles of Romantic thought. Unlike the Romantics, though, Dalziel and Scullion do not look back longingly to a 'Golden Age' in the past, to a sort of Garden of Eden unpolluted by modern society. Rather they look hopefully forward to a new and hoped-for synthesis between Nature and technology. They acknowledge in their work the awkward relationship between the two – how human technology can disrupt and potentially destroy Nature. Some of their works – *Modern Nature*, for example – reflect their fears. Some, such as *Voyager*, are ambivalent. But, ultimately,

the general tenor of their work is one of an informed and guarded optimism. If we can only learn to use modern technology to get closer to understanding Nature, there is hope for humanity. Dalziel and Scullion's work provides highly poetic and resonant metaphors for that closer relationship.

Notes

[1] Clement Greenberg, 'Modernist Painting' in *Arts Yearbook*, 1, New York, 1961; reprinted in Charles Harrison and Paul Wood, *Art in Theory 1900-1990*, Oxford, 1992 (pp. 754–760).

[2] Bruce Kurtz (ed), 'Conversation with Robert Smithson on April 22nd 1972', reprinted in Nancy Holt (ed.), *The Writings of Robert Smithson*, New York, 1979 (pp. 200–204).

[3] Scullion's fellow students in the Department of Environmental Art included Claire Barclay, Christine Borland, Roderick Buchanan, Nathan Coley, Douglas Gordon, Craig Richardson and Ross Sinclair.

[4] *The Gifted Child* was later remade for an exhibition in Rome, *New British Art*, curated by The British Council, in which the glass was suspended from a gallery ceiling.

[5] *General Release; Young British Artists at Scuola di San Pasquale, Venice, 1995*.

[6] John Muir, the ex-patriate Scot who had pioneered the movement to preserve the wildernesses of the United States in National Parks, became one of Dalziel and Scullion's favourite authors at this time.

Keith Hartley has been Senior Curator at the Scottish National Gallery of Modern Art since 1979. He studied German and French at Oxford University, and Art History at the Courtauld Institute, University of London and at Free University of Berlin. He has written widely, and curated exhibitions on Scottish, British, European and American art.

The Bathers 1993

The Bathers was commissioned by the Institute Français d'Ecosse as part of Fotofeis, the international festival of photography. The work consisted of three identical changing cubicles. At the rear of each compartment a super 8 film was projected onto a small etched circle on the glass, revealing different aspects of the sea.

Installation
Glass, wood, film
circa 2 x 3 x 1m

And so the "swimmer" has come gradually to represent characters with a heightened sensitivity to the promises of life, who are spiritually dissatisfied with worldly ambitions and find it hard to compromise. For the "swimmer" the ordered forms of everyday life seem inadequate and therefore intolerable.

The Haunt of the Black Masseur by Charles Sprawson

The Gifted Child 1995

The Gifted Child was originally commissioned by Visual Art Projects for an exhibition at Rouken Glen Park, an old Victorian park in Glasgow. A glass sheet was suspended from a mature birch tree. Video footage of the North Sea alternating with images of a synchronised swimmer were projected onto a 1.2m circular sandblasted area at the centre.

This work was later exhibited at the Centre for Contemporary Art, Glasgow, Ikon Gallery, Birmingham and the Stephania Miscetti Gallery, Rome.

Installation
Glass and video projection
2.4 x 2.1m

The Most Beautiful Thing 1995

Commissioned by The Scottish Arts Council Travelling Gallery, *The Most Beautiful Thing* consists of five large format photographs mounted in glass frames with a 10cm sandblasted border and five sets of scented text pieces. An edition of 5,000 of the texts were produced and distributed where the work was exhibited.

This work was toured by The Scottish Arts Council and later exhibited at Arnolfini, Bristol.

Photographs, glass, scented text
5 x (80 x 135 x 6cm)

Zhang

Edith

Valerie

Tim

Sargassum 1995

Sargassum was made for *General Release, Young British Artists* at the Scuola di San Pasquale as part of the Venice Biennale in 1995. A semi-transparent cloth was stretched between two parallel walls 9 metres long by 1.35 metres high, placed 3.3 metres apart. Arranged beneath the cloth were 50 blue light bulbs fitted with rotating discs, casting watery shadows on the cloth above.

Later shown at the Centre of Contemporary Art, Glasgow, The Ikon Gallery, Birmingham and Arnolfini, Bristol.

Installation
Painted timber, cloth, light bulbs, aluminium
1.35 x 9 x 3.3m
Fabrication by David McMillan

Wing 1996

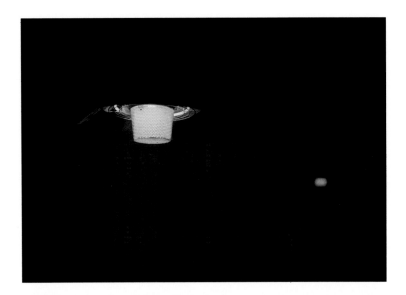

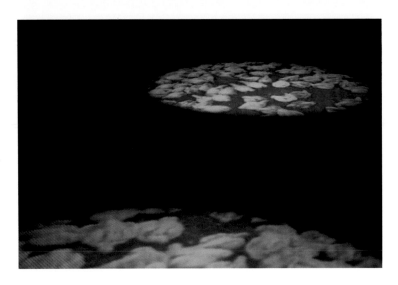

Funded by The Henry Moore Foundation for the Centre for Contemporary Art, Glasgow, *Wing* consisted of three circular floor projections with conical "brooder" heaters suspended overhead. The projected footage showed images from inside a commercial deep-litter chicken barn and was accompanied by an ambient sound track with sampled wild bird sounds.

The project later exhibited at The Ikon Gallery, Birmingham and Arnolfini, Bristol.

Installation
Heaters, video projection with sound
Size variable
Sound by Ray Chaston

Boulderstone by David Ward

The boulder stands in the gardens of West Park, near the centre of Wolverhampton, my home town, in the English Midlands. Irregular, rounded, weathered and worn, the old stone looks at odds with its cultivated surroundings. The rock appears placed, free-standing, like a sculpture. And as a sculpture might, it bears a plaque. From this I learned that this is a boulderstone, recognised by its geology as a stone carried for hundreds of miles to where it stands, by a glacier.

The boulder seized my imagination as a child. Its imposing weight seemed the sheer embodiment of gravity. I was impressed by this unformed block, forged by forces so extreme and yet so gradual that expressed such compression, abrasion and terrible cold. Above all was the captivating fact that it had come from elsewhere, from the north, carried within the glacial rubble, with excruciating, grinding, rumbling slowness.

The boulder came from the north, but more than that it was a physical part of the north, a piece of another place, a part of the world that I had never seen. Yet the stone transported me and I could picture a place from which it had moved, invisibly, within the ice.

The boulder had arrived there not with the spectacular spark of a meteorite but with an imperceptible, yet irresistible progress, reminiscent of 'The Convergence of the Twain'. In this poem Thomas Hardy imagined the formation of the iceberg that was to collide with the Titanic. Hardy described it as:

> *A Shape of Ice, for the time far and dissociate:*
> *And as the smart ship grew*
> *In stature, grace and hue,*
> *In shadowy silent distance grew the Iceberg too.*

But the violence of the boulderstone's formation ebbed away with the recession of the glacier of which it had been a part. Now it stands still, both in my memory and in the park, with a mute inevitability and resigned presence, a resilient reminder of the persistence of the natural world.

The boulder transforms the park, or rather it enables a glimpse of another landscape, a previous or pre-existing land. My fantasy has always been that the boulder was never moved from where it lay after the glacier withdrew, an erratic deposit that remained unchanged while all around it altered: the coming of the forests and their felling; the cutting and dressing of other stones and their removal for building; sheep perhaps grazing around the rock before being herded into the folds of the nearby town.

The boulder stood unhewn through all this as the land around it was worked, fields tilled, iron smelted, coal mined, canals cut, roads laid, homes built and then the planting of the park as the town spread out all around. All of this I imagined occurring with the boulder never shifting from its spot, a permanent punctuation.

The boulder represents an archaic point, unchanged by time, in the midst of the modern world. Hardy had described a fateful collision between modernity and nature, polarised as *two hemispheres* yet drawn together by *paths coincident*. As Rainer Maria Rilke looked ahead into the twentieth century he wrote of the relationship between art and the modern world suggesting that …*what distinguishes works of art from all other objects is that they are, as it were, things of the future, things whose time has not yet come.*

He continues:

> *Our lamps have finally become far-sighted, our instruments reach beyond tomorrow and the day after, with the methods of research we extract coming centuries from the future and make them into a kind of not-yet-begun present. Science has unfolded like a long road with no discernible end; the hard and painful progress of mankind, both of individuals and the masses, fills the coming millennia like some endless, laborious task.*

> *And far, far beyond all that lies the home of works of art, those strangely secretive and patient objects, which have their existence among the things of everyday use, among busy human beings, working beasts and playing children.*

The boulder still stands, patiently, in the gardens of the park.

David Ward is an artist. He has been artist-in-residence at King's College, Cambridge (1991), Harvard University (1994) and Durham Cathedral (1997-98), and was a Research Fellow at the Henry Moore Institute, Leeds (1995). He has taught at a number of institutions including Goldsmiths' College, London (1988-95) and Glasgow School of Art (1995-97), and currently teaches at the Architectural Association, London. He has written about and curated the work of other artists, notably for *The British Art Show* in 1990. Recent solo exhibitions include installations at Durham Cathedral and the Royal Festival Hall in 2000. During 2000/2001 he has completed permanent works in Bristol, Coventry, Lowestoft and Wolverhampton.

TORN

The Horn 1997

The Horn was commissioned by West Lothian Council for the M8 Motorway, which runs between Glasgow and Edinburgh. The structure, which can be seen from one mile in each direction, is designed to broadcast short audio messages to passing traffic at random intervals. It has a lifespan of 25 years, during which the sounds will be continually updated. Travellers are invited to exit the motorway at junctions 4 or 5 to hear *The Horn* speak.

The project was managed by Art in Partnership, Edinburgh and funded by a Scottish Arts Council National Lottery award.

Sculptura/sound installation
Stainless steel, concrete base
24m high

Structural Design by Halcrow Crouch, Glasgow
Fabrication by Solway Engineering, Galloway

Top: foghorn, Kinnaird Head, north east Scotland
Bottom: cows crossing motorway on elevated farm track

Migrator 1997

Migrator was commissioned by BAA for the New World Business Centre at Heathrow Airport. Birdcalls of migratory Scottish wild birds were broadcast to pan across the main atrium area of the building. Footage of an endless sea journey is shown on two television monitors positioned in the entrance foyer.

Installation with sound
8 speakers, 2 x 23" monitors on stands

Endlessly 1997

Endlessly was commissioned by the Northern Gallery for Contemporary Art in Sunderland for an exhibition entitled *Luminous*. The work consisted of two large screens with back-projected videos. On one screen is the image of a stone angel from a graveyard filmed from dawn till dusk and speeded up to 30 minutes. The second projection shows the continuous motion of the surface of the sea. The work is accompanied by a sound track of an oscillating wave pattern with ambient sounds.

Endlessly was part of the North East of England's Year of Visual Art in 1996. The work was later shown during the Edinburgh Festival at the Scottish National Gallery of Modern Art, Edinburgh, in 1997.

Installation
Painted timber structures with video and sound
Angel: 2.4 x 4.1 x 0.6m
Sea: 2.6 x 2.4 x 2.3m (including ramp)
Sound by Ray Chaston
Fabrication by David Macmillan and Andy Miller

Goes Ah 1997

First shown at Iain Irving Projects, Peterhead, Aberdeenshire. Three images taken from a moving car were mounted in curved light-boxes. The work was accompanied by sound sampled from radio broadcasts and other media, combining ideas and images about art, location and environment. In the gallery space, the soundtracks initially converge but gradually separate as individual lightboxes are approached.

Also shown at An Tuireann Arts Centre on the Isle of Skye in 1998.

Installation with sound
Light-boxes, duratran images
3 x (30 x 42cm)

Driven 2001

Re-working of *Goes Ah*, commissioned by Yorkshire Sculpture Park in 2001
as a larger scale work with additional images.

Installation with sound
Lightboxes, duratrans
4 x (56 x 84cm)

The Way Stations 1997

The Way Stations was commissioned by Duff House, Aberdeenshire, Australian Centre for Contemporary Art, Melbourne and Artconnexion, Lille. Seven small architectural models were photographed in a variety of settings, each image depicting particular themes of human activity.

Also exhibited at The Pier Art Centre in Stromness, Orkney.

Photographic installation
Seven images printed on vinyl
Size varies from 0.6 x 0.7m to 2.5 x 3m

A Less Remote Place: Art Ecology and Dalziel + Scullion by Judith Findlay

It is an ordinary weekday evening. The children are in bed. The baby is also asleep, between feeds. This is when, like parents everywhere, after a hectic day filled relentlessly (gloriously, noisily) to the brim with childish and domestic concerns, I am able to spend some time on other things: watching a film, listening to music, reading a book or magazine, writing. These are things I used to do much more before becoming a parent – before, when I was involved in 'work' and 'art', not 'home' and 'domesticity'; when, in retrospect, I had time enough to spare. These days things have changed a lot. Priorities and desires have altered. Perspectives and foci have shifted. Art (and writing about art) has become a little more marginal – or at least not as central to my life as it once was. Tonight though, I am leafing through some articles about the artists Matthew Dalziel and Louise Scullion. They and their work seem somehow relevant to my present situation.

The concepts of 'distance' and 'marginality' – if you like, the *home-life* of Dalziel and Scullion – have always seemed relevant for an understanding of the artists' practice, even as their practice has provided a way of understanding the concept of 'not being central'. Thus, Dalziel and Scullion's 'remoteness' – the fact that for most of their careers they have lived and worked at a distance from cities, and therefore from the 'art world' – previously seemed important, and therefore worth mentioning.[1] Their situation, living in a small fishing cottage in the village of St Combs on the north east coast of Scotland, had a special significance. It seemed to mark them out as different, and even had an exotic appeal.

But Dalziel and Scullion now live in Dundee – a city, an art world, a place that is less remote. The question is: has the act of moving 'nearer' changed Dalziel and Scullion's work? Has their shift changed the work's distinction, its appeal?

Previously the geography in which Dalziel and Scullion chose to locate themselves – the landscape (and seascape) that they took as their reference – seemed intrinsic to their work. This place, deemed 'outside' art, combines and confuses the natural and the man-made, the ancient and the modern. It is flat and stark (some might say bleak): an environment of 'Edward Hopper' light; of long, deserted beaches and white lighthouses ; of strange, modern installations related to oil, gas, farming, fishing and national defence – a fascinating 'non-art' place that seemed important to write about, and to identify artistically. This was where, for ten years, Dalziel and Scullion lived and worked, where they filmed, recorded and

photographed, walked and drove, sat and gazed, gained source material, imagery, information, and inspiration. *The Bathers, Sargassum, The Gifted Child, The Most Beautiful Thing, Wing* and *The Horn* are a few of the art works conceived here. Rattray Head, Macduff, the Loch of Strathbeg, St Fergus, Crimond Airfield, Cruden Bay — these are some of the wonderful names that pinpoint places where Dalziel and Scullion made these and other works, as well as models of and for ideas, sometimes to be shown 'here' and at other times to be shown 'elsewhere'. These places and their peoples seemed to be what their work was about; what identified it. For me this was absolutely 'the lure of the local'[2], or, more accurately, the lure of the local seen through artistic eyes. Even as I sifted through and listed these 'invisible' places (in art journals, catalogues and the like) I caused them to become visible. As Jonathan Bate and Lucy Lippard respectively point out: 'to name a place is to allow that place its being.'[3] 'Every place name is a story, an outcropping of the shared tales that form the bedrock of community. Untold land is unknown land.'[4] In other words, by naming these places within artistic networks they were given artistic meaning, however 'romantic' or *created*. For a time they were given artistic identities.

This point then highlights something interesting both about 'remoteness' in general, and about Dalziel and Scullion's 'artistic remoteness' specifically. And, before I further alienate all the many excellent practitioners who do actually live and work in this so called artistic wilderness — the artists, curators, gallery owners, administrators, researchers, organisers and writers — I should stress that it also underlines the way in which the concept of 'remoteness' might be 'spun', represented or indeed misrepresented.

As the dictionary tells us, meanings of the word 'remote' include 'distantly related or connected' and 'aloof or abstracted'. Yet what becomes clear on scrutiny of Dalziel and Scullion's back catalogue is that for all their 'remoteness' they were (and are) very well connected indeed. What also becomes apparent is that they were 'rooted' — not aloof or abstracted, but rather in touch with and sensitive to the material, the concrete, the practical and the personal. They were, to use Bate's words again, not concerned with obtaining a picturesque view of things so much as involving themselves in 'an exploration of the inter-relatedness of perception and creation [and engaging in] a meditation on the *networks* which link mental and environmental space.'[5] This further suggests then that even as they were rooted or *located*, they were, at the same time, not fixed. They were mobile, and they travelled (intellectually as well as physically). Now they have moved, and have recently travelled to northern Scandinavia in search of new source material. It seems a good time then to write about Dalziel and Scullion's work again — to look at it in a new light and context. To return to the earlier question, has their change of location and scrutiny of different places altered their work? Has it changed what originally drew me to them and their practice?

It is possible to answer 'yes' and 'no'. Yes, of course their work is now about different landscapes. In a way this does change what, for me, was a definite pull of their work: seen through Dalziel and Scullion's eyes, the north east coast of Aberdeenshire *is* attractive. And yes, they and their work are no longer characterised by being 'far away'. However, more interesting than this – and more important – is the fact that their relocation doesn't change Dalziel and Scullion's fundamental concerns, or my joy in their work, at all. Somehow their move highlights these interests, these pleasures – it improves and develops them. It occurs to me that, even if the attraction of the artists' work may be to do with how they see and experience a particular place, the value of their research lies in their enquiry into, and interpretation of, the nature of places as 'hybrids' or 'amalgams' of many different locations[6]. For in reality a sense of place simultaneously combines experiences of 'here' and 'there', 'now and 'then', our imagining of a place and our experience of what it actually is. To quote Doreen Massey:

'…it seems that you can sense the simultaneous presence of everywhere in the place where you are standing. Conceptualised in terms of the geography of social relations, what is happening is that the social relations which constitute a locality increasingly stretch beyond its borders; less and less of these relations are contained within the place itself.'[7]

Which suggests that, as Francois Matarasso puts it:

'…the very notion of remoteness… is itself a polarity, inseparable from its counterpart, because it is defined by its relationship to something characterised as its centre… So we should be careful with this interesting concept of the edge and keep in mind that one person's margin may be another's heartland.'[8]

Thus, it was not Dalziel and Scullion's 'remoteness' *per se* that was interesting, but rather the connections – and the social relations – that they made from, interjected into and cultivated within that 'remoteness'. While one must undoubtedly recognise the beauty of their aesthetic, and the richness of their content, clearly one has to acknowledge what might be called the 'worth of their method'. This has something to do with a perception of the particularities of their immediate surroundings (which Thomas Hardy describes as 'local knowledge') coupled with a knowledge and imagining of 'elsewhere'. Which is to say that 'remoteness' is relative. The question is: remote to what?

At this point, one might discuss the way in which 'remoteness' is becoming 'less remote'. One could debate, for example, issues of globalisation, developments in technology, instantaneous worldwide communication and the apparent 'break-up of what were once local coherencies, and a new and violent phase of "time space compression".'[19] These are all things that Dalziel and Scullion have shown an interest in. But what interests me more here is something related, but simultaneously more abstract and straightforward. What I want to highlight is this notion of *connections*.

If 'connections' and 'social relations' are the concepts we must hold on to, then it seems to me that words such as 'remoteness', 'here' and 'there', 'near' and 'far' – at least as far as Dalziel and Scullion are concerned – just won't do. I want to propose then that a different term is used – one that embodies the concept of 'connections'. The term that I propose is *ecology*, or more specifically, *art ecology*.

What might the basics of 'art ecology' be, and what might its beginnings mean in terms of the work of Dalziel and Scullion? In the first instance, one might focus on Dalziel and Scullion's concerns for the environment, for landscape and the 'natural'. One might examine their interest in the ways in which humans interact with nature (and with the *idea* of nature). One could, for instance, look at a work such as *Modern Nature,* with its Capercaillie call, in terms of conservation and extinction. One might examine the flight of birds juxtaposed with the need of human beings to move fast and far around the globe by referring to *Migrator.* Or one might study the pros and cons of human forays into 'wilderness' as implied by *Voyager:* the compulsion of people to travel, and to explore new places – to take risks – coupled with the awareness that the 'purity' of these places is then changed for ever.

As Bate stresses, '...ecology... emphasizes the interconnectedness of all things'. As (art) ecologists, it could be argued that Dalziel and Scullion make art works that imply the completeness of a living earth that requires and thrives on the 'intricacy and precision of its interconnected working parts – winds, currents, rocks, plants, animals, weathers...'[10.] In essence, therefore, Dalziel and Scullion make art works that show a care for the world.

More than this though, their care (their art ecology) comprises concern for a whole living *cultural* world; they emphasise a world that is interconnected and made dynamic by *cultural* working parts. Television and radio, films and music, architecture and design, the media and consumerism, literature and, of course, art – these and the images and objects, rituals, relationships, practices, perceptions, needs and beliefs that embody people's everyday lives influence and inspire their work. In other words, their work thrives on the interconnectedness of nature and culture. It is an ecological art, and also an artistic ecology.[11] Crucially, then, the move from the country to the city was not so very great, because it seems that Dalziel and Scullion have always examined (and revelled in) how these interrelate. They have involved themselves in an exploration of the ways in which any given place is a hybrid of the rural and the urban.

Dalziel and Scullion use and make conspicuous an ecological perception that acknowledges what might be called a 'landscape narrative'[12]. This narrative recognises that humans must (positively) take their place alongside other things in nature, just as art must take its place alongside other things in culture. One is involved in a journey – a journey in and through a landscape that is both real and conceptual. It is a story that is cultural as much as it is natural, urban as much as it is rural, central as much as it is remote, and domestic as much as it is non-domestic.

This brings me to another point about ecology: it implies a connection with home-life (with dwelling, and how one lives in the world).[13] This seems entirely apt with regard to Dalziel and Scullion, because they stress the rituals of daily lives – not only within their artworks, but actually in terms of (*contained within*) the everyday. It is not just that I can visit and view their artworks in galleries and other public places. It is not only that I can buy and own their multiples (or even that I have a couple of their works here in my house). It is more to do with how they imply that simple, mundane tasks and routines are in themselves art – and in a sense then their art doesn't necessarily rely on the mediation of an artwork. Thus, for example, the brewing of coffee, an orange held up against a blue sky, the buying and wearing of perfume, the eating of an

apple, a family photograph, an electric fire, the lighting of a candle, a drive in a car, a recipe, a walk, a thought or a memory can become art.

So as I sit here surrounded by TV and toys, the debris of lunch and 'messy time' still on the kitchen table, my sons packed off in the car so that I can finish this essay, my baby daughter about to waken and demand attention, the ecology of Dalziel and Scullion seems appropriate for me too. For it provides a way of shedding light on my situation – of making where I am   (and perhaps where others like me are) *artistically* relevant. It offers 'genuine continuity'[14] between art and home-life. Domesticity *is* worth mentioning – in terms of art it *is* significant. Moreover, as Rita Felski has pointed out, 'the boundaries between home and non-home are leaky'[15]. Home is a hybrid, an amalgam as well. So even as the world of art may sometimes seem remote to me now, Dalziel and Scullion's story – their 'narrative of artistic interaction' – is one in which I can find a place. Just as it 'defies the mundane' (takes me out of myself, puts me somewhere else),[16] it also recreates, and *reconnects* the mundane (everyday routines, social contexts and social experiences) as, and with, something special, something transcendent. It brings me nearer.

Notes

[1] See for example my interview with Dalziel and Scullion: Judith Findlay, 'Matthew Dalziel and Louise Scullion: An Interview with Judith Findlay', in <u>Art & Design</u> (Profile No. 46, Public Art), 1996, pp. 17-23.

2 See Lucy Lippard, *The Lure of the Local* (The New Press: New York, 1997).

3 Jonathan Bate, *The Song of the Earth*, (Picador: London, 2000), p. 175.

4 Ibid, Lucy Lippard, p. 46.

5 Ibid, Jonathan Bate, p. 148.

6 See Angelika Bammer, 'Editorial', <u>New Formations</u>, no. 17 (summer, 1992); and Doreen Massey, 'A Place Called Home', <u>New Formations</u>, no. 17 (summer, 1992).

7 Ibid, Doreen Massey, p. 7.

8 Francois Matarasso, 'On the Edge: Art, Culture and Rural Communities', conference paper, Duff House, Aberdeenshire, 31 May, 2001 (unpublished).

9 Ibid, Doreen Massey, p. 3.

10 Ibid, Jonathan Bate, p. 27.

11 There are precedents for bringing culture and ecology together. Jonathan Bate's project of linking literature and ecology is one, Neil Postman's is another. Having coined the term 'media ecology', he offers this description:
'Media ecology looks into the matter of how media communication affect human perception, understanding, feeling and value; and how our interaction with media facilitates or impedes our chances of survival. The word ecology implies the study of environments: their structure, content and impact on people. An environment is, after all, a complex message system which imposes on human beings certain ways of thinking, feeling and behaving.'
Neil Postman, 'The Reformed English Curriculum', in Alvin C. Eurich (ed.), <u>High School 1980: The Shape of the Future in American Secondary Education</u> (Pitman: New York, 1970), p.161.

12 Lippard describes landscape as 'hermetic narrative': "Finding a fitting place for oneself in the world is finding a place for oneself in a story". The story is composed of mythologies, histories, ideologies – the stuff of identity and representation.' (See Lucy Lippard, ibid, p. 33).

13 The word 'ecology' – the prefix 'eco' – is derived from Greek *oikos*, meaning 'home or place of dwelling'.

14 See Colin Painter, <u>The Uses of an Artist: Constable in Constable Country Now</u> (Ipswich: Ipswich Borough Council Museums and Galleries, 1998) and Colin Painter, <u>At Home With Art</u> (London: Hayward Gallery Publishing, 1999).

15 Rita Felski, 'The Invention of Everyday Life', <u>New Formations</u>, no. 39, p. 24.

16 See Simon Frith, <u>Performing Rites: On the Value of Popular Music</u> (Oxford, New York: Oxford University Press, 1996), p. 275.

Judith Findlay is a writer who lives in the village of Catterline in Aberdeenshire. Her PhD, titled 'Fine Art as Performance', is an anthropological study of visual art. She has written for numerous publications, the most recent being the journals 'Critical Quarterly' and '292: Essays in Visual Culture'. She is married to Iain Irving and has three children, Leon, Ben and Hester.

The Pressure of Spring 1999

The Pressure of Spring was
commissioned by Channel Four
Television as part of the series of
short films by new directors
entitled *Documentary Lab*. Made
on location in the north east of
Scotland, the film examines the
lives of young people from a rural
environment.

11 minute film
Broadcast August 1999
Nominated for Best Director,
New Talent BAFTA Award 2000
Music by Howie B

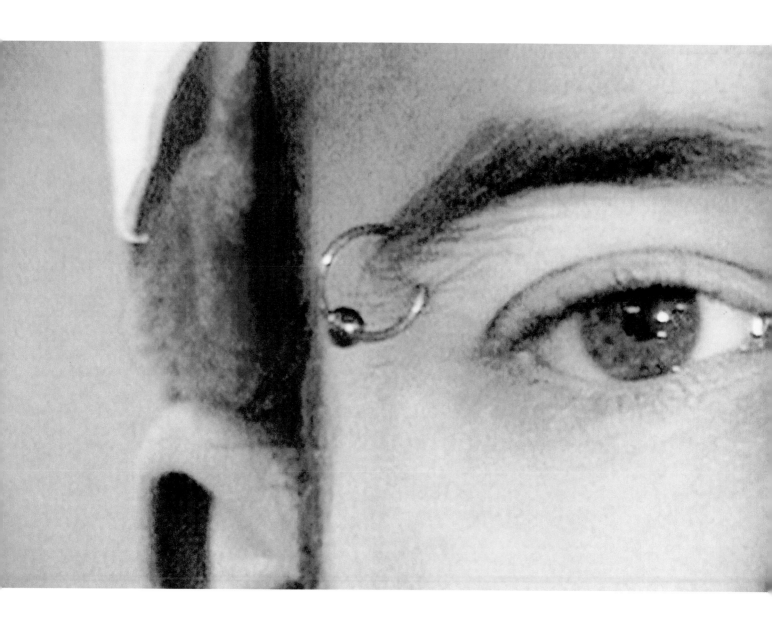

Another Place 2000

Another Place is a series of video portraits filmed in the north east of Scotland that considered a non-urban way of life. The film is slowed down to a fifth of its original speed, and is accompanied by an ambient soundtrack.

The work was first conceived for Lisbon Expo in 1997, and later reworked for Glasgow Gallery of Modern Art in 2000. It was purchased for the collection of Aberdeen Art Gallery, and has also exhibited at The National Maritime Museum, London.

Installation
16 minute video projection with sound, size variable
Sound by Ray Chaston

Rain 2000

Rain was commissioned by Oriel 31 in Newtown, Wales. The structure was conceived as a temporary pavilion for the contemplation of rain. A tin roof amplified the sound of falling rain, and channelled it into a collecting pool at the rear. The pavilion was entered by a long wooden ramp, and a simple bench was provided for visitors. The walls of the structure were clad in a cellular plastic material, which reflected a luminous quality of light during daylight hours. In the evening the structure was lit by an animated gobo system that created a stylised pattern of rain on the walls.

Installation
Wood, plastic, tin
5 x 5 x 5m structure, 6 x 6m pool, 1.5 x 5m ramp
Technical design by Acanthas Architects
Fabrication by Elm Developments

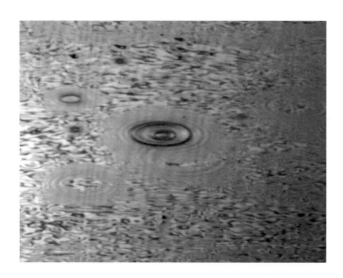

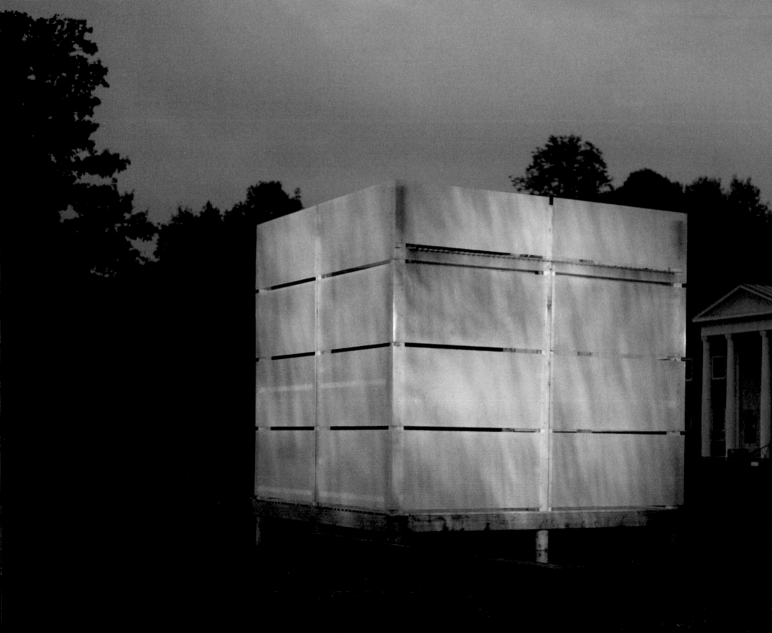

Modern Nature 2000

Modern Nature was commissioned by the Tyrebagger Trust for Elrick Hill, north of Aberdeen. The work consists of six tall aluminium structures, grouped like a glade of silver birch, which house solar panels powering a sound system. The speakers, buried underground in the surrounding landscape, periodically broadcast the call of the male Capercaillie.

Installation
Aluminium structures, solar panels, sound system
6 structures, each 5m high
Managed by Art in Partnership, Edinburgh
Sound installation by A&M Sound

Sanctuary Furniture 2001

Work commissioned by Artlink's Fusion project for the Edinburgh Royal
Infirmary Sanctuary. The work comprises a beech wood table with
coloured glass insert under which rhythmic patterns of light are visible. The
work is accompanied by two long freestanding lamps, each with printed
photographic drop paper shades.

Installation
Beech table 56 x 80 x 60cm
Two lamps, each 173 x 21cm

Meltwater 2001

Three part photographic and film installation commissioned for Sadler's Wells, London. The work comprises *Path,* a circular image of a path to a glacier printed onto a 10 metre drop of canvas. This curtain fell through three floors in the foyer area of the theatre. It also includes *Valley,* four lozenge-shaped images of trees perched on precarious stone ledges which were displayed on padded timber frames. *Ice Stream* features video footage of green, silt-heavy meltwater, filmed flowing from the glacier. This footage was displayed on public information screens.

Photographic installation
Path: 10 x 7m (image 6m diameter) on digital canvas
Valley: 4 photographic images on digital canvas, each 3 x 1m
Ice Stream: 4 x 15min looped digital videos

Voyager 2001

Three two-person expedition tents cast in aluminium. Exhibited outdoors at Yorkshire Sculpture Park (above) and later as an indoor installation on a scree of industrial ash.

Voyager was commissioned by Yorkshire Sculpture Park in collaboration with The Fruitmarket Gallery, Edinburgh, Milton Keynes Gallery and Manchester Art Gallery. The work was sponsored by Powderhall Bronze, Edinburgh.

Installation
Cast aluminium tents
3 tents, each 1.2 x 3.4 x 1m
Precasting by A.P.E. Cunningham & McKay
Casting by Powderhall Bronze

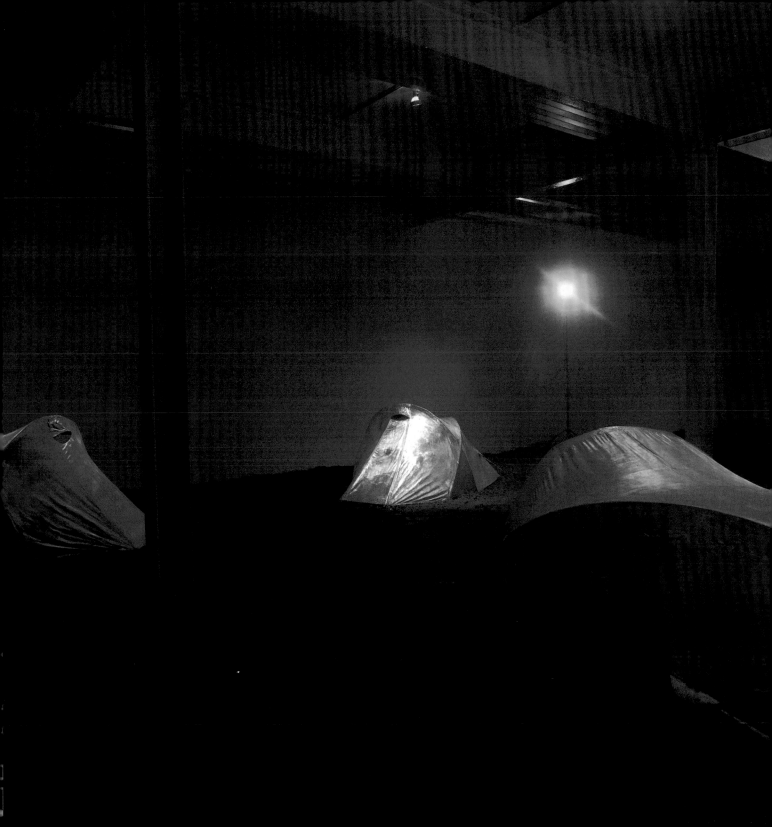

Drift 2001

Six part work, comprising four upright and two horizontal images describing the animated forces that created the glacial valley of Jostedalsbreen in Norway. The images commence in the fertile woods at the valley bottom, working up to the moraine fields and to the glacier itself.

Drift was commissioned by The Fruitmarket Gallery, Edinburgh, in collaboration with Milton Keynes Gallery and Manchester Art Gallery as part of the exhibition *Home*.

Photographic installation
Freestanding photographic prints on digital canvas stretched over timber frames. Clad at rear with dressed birch plywood.
Variable sizes, from 3 x 4 x 0.5m to 0.2 x 4 x 1.75m
Fabrication of timber frames and backing by Malcolm Cheyne and Jason Nelson.

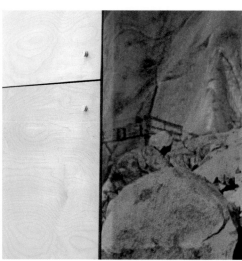

Habitat 2001

Habitat features a tightly framed group of penguins filmed in a constructed habitat of concrete 'nests' and boulders in Bergen Akvarium, Norway. The footage of the penguins is projected within the context of a domestic interior featuring armchairs and a carpet. The work is accompanied by an ambient sound track.

Habitat was commissioned by The Fruitmarket Gallery, Edinburgh, in collaboration with Milton Keynes Gallery and Manchester Art Gallery as part of the exhibition *Home*.

15 minute video installation
Sound by Gerald Mair

Water Falls Down 2001

Film constructed in three parts. The first part commences with a view of a large boulder over which a torrent of water is flowing. The middle section shows a scene from a baptism at sea filmed near the village of St. Combs in north east Scotland. The last section concludes with the view of a birch sapling in a heavy fall of snow.

Water Falls Down was commissioned by The Fruitmarket Gallery, Edinburgh in collaboration with Milton Keynes Gallery and Manchester Art Gallery as part of the exhibition *Home*.

Video installation, 9 minutes and 24 seconds
Sound by Geir Jenssen

Postcard 2001

Film footage of 'outstanding view points' in Norway projected to the size of a postcard. The scenes depicted vary from glacial mountain ranges to 'Nature Park' visitor centres.

Postcard was commissioned by The Fruitmarket Gallery, Edinburgh in collaboration with Milton Keynes Gallery and Manchester Art Gallery as part of the exhibition *Home*.

Video installation, 8 minutes

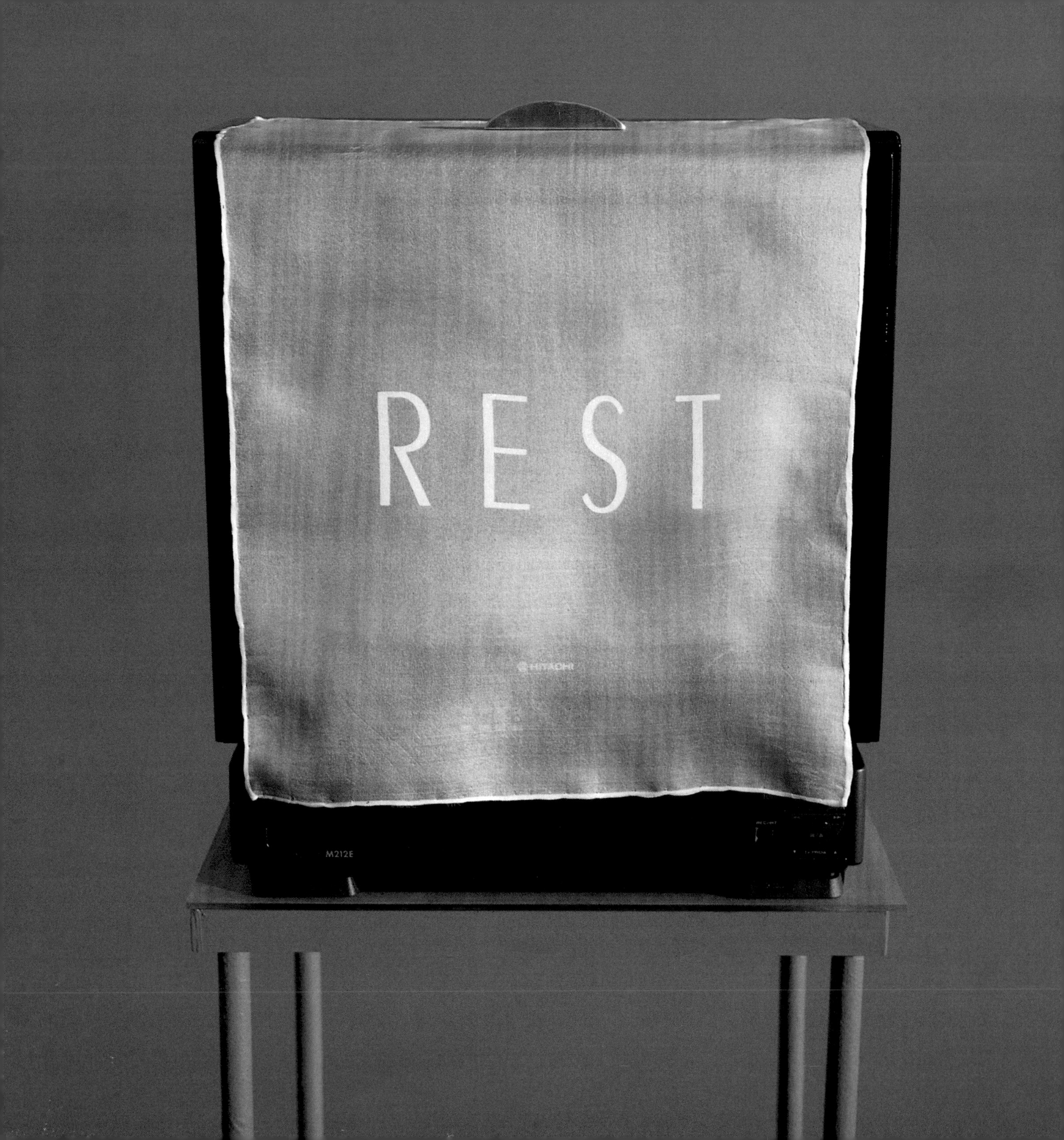
REST
HITACHI
M212E

Rest 1995

Printed, semi-transparent cloth with a small, polished metal holding weight, designed to veil a television screen when not in use. Made to fit 14" and 21" screens.

This work was commissioned by the South Bank Centre, London and the Centre for Contemporary Art, Glasgow to be one of ten new multiples in the exhibition *Art Unlimited: Multiples from the 1960s and 1990s from the Arts Council's Collection.*

Installation
Roll hemmed silk organza and aluminium weight
14": 50 x 42cm
21": 60 x 50cm

Behind the veil lay the holy place where the ark was situated, and where the very presence of God resided

Imperial Bible Dictionary

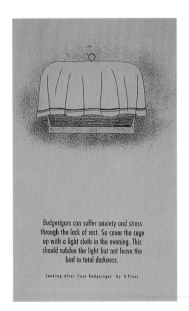

Budgerigars can suffer anxiety and stress through the lack of rest. So cover the cage up with a light cloth in the evening. This should subdue the light but not leave the bird in total darkness.

Looking After Your Budgerigar by H Piers

Endless Sea 1996

A satellite work taken from the continuous sea
footage of the work *Endlessly*. Made as an ambient
work for domestic television.

Multiple
3 hour VHS tape and packaging
Edition of 200

Lost Wave 1997

First shown at Iain Irving Projects, Peterhead,
Aberdeenshire. Clear plastic beach ball containing
500ml water collected from within the 2km
exclusion zone around Douneray Nuclear Power
Station.

Also shown at The Morioka Hashimoto Museum
of Art, Japan and The Contemporary Art Space,
Christchurch, New Zealand.

Multiple
Seawater and plastic beach ball, 50cm diameter
Edition of 80

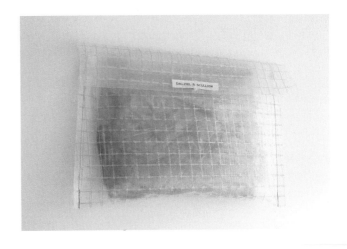

Out There 1998

Postcard featuring an image of a mobile phone being thrown into the North Sea (opposite). On the reverse of the card is the mobile telephone number that can be called by the recipient of the card.

Postcard
11 x 17cm
edition of 1,000
Commissioned by Coil, Journal of the Moving & Photographic Image

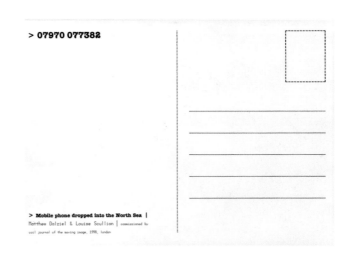

> 07970 077382

> Mobile phone dropped into the North Sea |
Matthew Dalziel & Louise Scullion | commissioned by
coil journal of the moving image, 1998, london

The Idea of North 1998

Boxed work consisting of a compass embedded in a disc of sandblasted perspex with etched text and colours.

Multiple
Engraved perspex disc and compass
11 x 11 x 1.5cm (boxed)
Edition of 200
Commissioned by the Multiple Store, London

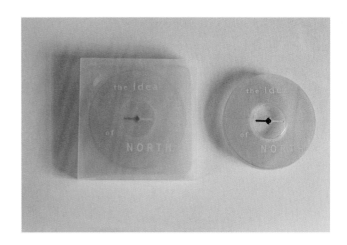

Biographies

MATTHEW DALZIEL

1957   Born Irvine, Scotland

Education
1981-85   BA (Hons) Fine Art, Duncan of Jordanstone College of Art and Design, Dundee
1985-87   Gwent College of Higher Education, Wales
1987-88   Glasgow School of Art, MA in Sculpture and Fine Art Photography

Exhibitions & Commissions
1987   *Forces*, Gwent College of Art, University College Cardiff
1988   *Mysterious Coincidences*, London, Cardiff, California, Hong Kong & Melbourne
1989   *Ways of Telling*, Oriel Mostyn Gallery, Llandudno
        Unseen, Unheard of But Measured, St. Fergus Gas Plant, Peterhead
        Through Photography, Third Eye Centre, Glasgow
1990   *Artists in Industry*, Aberdeen Art Gallery
        The British Art Show, McLellan Gallery, Glasgow, Leeds City Art Centre and the Hayward Gallery, London
        1st International Event Symposium, Tokyo
        Either/Or, Kelvingrove Art Gallery, St. Enoch Shopping Centre, Billboard Art Works, Glasgow
1992   *Blue & White*, commissioned by Tramway, Glasgow
        Everything is True, commissioned by Cambridge Darkroom and Addenbrooke's Hospital, Cambridge
        Satellites & Monuments, large scale light work commissioned by Lux Europae, Edinburgh

LOUISE SCULLION

1966   Born Helensburgh, Scotland

Education
1984-88   BA (Hons) Fine Art, Glasgow School of Art

Exhibitions & Commissions
1987   *Reconnaissance Bench*, commissioned by the Glasgow Garden Festival
        Just Another Outdoor Game, Third Eye Centre, Glasgow
1989   *Scatter*, Third Eye Centre, Glasgow
        Wonder, Smith Art Gallery & Museum, Stirling
1990   *The British Art Show*, McLellan Gallery, Glasgow, Leeds City Art Centre and the Hayward Gallery, London
        Mapping the Interior, Scottish Arts Council Tour
        The Lie of the Land, Compass Gallery, Glasgow
        Four Contemporary Sculptors, the Bluecoat Gallery, Liverpool
1991   *Iris*, An Laintair Gallery, Stornoway
        Speed, Transmission Gallery, Glasgow
1992   *The Furnished Landscape*, Crafts Council Gallery, London
        Vending Machines, commissioned by Lux Europae, Edinburgh

DALZIEL + SCULLION

Solo Projects

1995   *The Most Beautiful Thing*, Scottish Arts Council
Commission for the Travelling Gallery
Dalziel + Scullion, Centre for Contemporary Art,
Glasgow and Ikon Gallery, Birmingham

1996   *British Waves – New British Art in Rome*, Studio Miscetti,
Rome, as part of a British Festival of Arts
Dalziel + Scullion, Arnolfini Gallery, Bristol

1997   *Goes Ah*, Iain Irving Projects, Aberdeenshire
Endlessly, Scottish National Gallery of Modern Art,
Edinburgh
Migrator, permanent work commissioned for the World
Business Centre, Heathrow Airport, London
The Horn, permanent work commissioned by West
Lothian Council for the M8 Motorway

1998   *The Way Stations*, Centre for Contemporary Art,
Melbourne, Australia

1999   *The Way Stations*, Art Connexion, Lille, France, Duff
House, Banff (project commissioner) and The Pier Art
Centre, Orkney
The Pressure of Spring, short film commissioned by
Channel Four Television

2000   *Modern Nature*, commissioned permanent work for
Elrick Hill in the north east of Scotland
Rain, Oriel 31 Gallery, Powys, Wales
BAFTA New Talent Scotland, nomination for Best Film
Director for *The Pressure of Spring* (Channel 4, 1999)

2001   *Voyager*, Yorkshire Sculpture Park, Wakefield
Meltwater, Sadler's Wells Theatre, London
Becquerel's Tree, new work commissioned for Nicholas
Grimshaw Building: *Millenium Point*, Birmingham
Bell, work in progress for Yesnaby Cliffs, Orkney
(project organiser The Pier Art Centre, Orkney)

Selected Group Exhibitions

1993   *Public and Private*, Institut Francais d'Ecosse as part of
Fotofeis '95

1994   *4 Minutes*, commissioned permanent work for the
Science Museum, London
*Art Unlimited: Multiples of the 1960s and 1990s from the
British Arts Council Collection*, South Bank Centre,
London

1995   *Arts Beast*, outdoor film installation commissioned for
Rouken Glen Park, Glasgow
*Venice Biennale, Young British Artists at Scuola di San
Pasquale*
Swarm, Scottish Arts Council Travelling Gallery
Shadows on the Water, Fotofeis international touring
exhibition

1996   *Luminous*, Northern Gallery of Contemporary Art,
Sunderland
Girl's High, Old Fruitmarket, Glasgow

1997   *If it wasn't for the mist we could see your home across the
bay...*, Grays School of Art, Aberdeen
Fast Moving Car, Iain Irving Projects, Peterhead,
Aberdeenshire
Lisbon Expo 97, three films commissioned for National
Day for Britain

1998   *Exhibition of British Multiples*, The Morioka Hashimoto
Museum of Art, Japan
This Island Earth, An Tuireann, Isle of Skye, Scotland
Scottish Contemporary Artists, The Contemporary Art
Space, Christchurch, New Zealand
Out There, postcard work for inclusion in *Coil*, Journal of
the Moving Image, London
The Idea of North, edition of 200 compasses for the
Multiple Store, London

2000   *Infinatude*, Gallery of Modern Art, Glasgow
        The Idea of North, Leeds City Arts Centre
2001   *New Visions of the Sea*, National Maritime Museum,
        London
        The Forum, Norwich Gallery, Norwich
        Here and Now, McManus Gallery, Dundee
        Contemporary Arts, Generator and Aberdeen Art
        Gallery, Scotland
        Shriek From an Invisible Box, Merguro Museum of Art,
        Tokyo
        Re-mote, Photographer's Gallery, London

Selected Publications

1987   *Mysterious Coincidences*, Photographers Gallery, London
1989   *Ways of Telling*, Oriel Mosten Gallery, Llandudno, Wales
        Scatter, The Third Eye Centre, Glasgow
        Through Photography, The Third Eye Centre, Glasgow
1990   *The British Art Show 4*, South Bank Centre, London
1992   *Power and Providence*, Cambridge Darkroom,
        Cambridge
        Lux Europae, published to coincide with European
        Summit art exhibition, Edinburgh
1995   *The Most Beautiful Thing – Dalziel + Scullion*, Scottish
        Arts Council, Edinburgh
1995   *Desire and the work of Dalziel + Scullion*, Red Bluff
        Young British Artists at Scuola di San Pasquale, Venice
        Biennale, The British Council, London
        Small Living Things That Fly, CCA, Glasgow
        Shadows in the Water, Fotofeis Ltd, Scotland
1996   *British Artists in Rome*, The British Council, Rome
        Luminous, Northern Gallery for Contemporary Art,
        Sutherland
1997   *Endlessly*, Scottish National Gallery of Modern Art,
        Edinburgh

1997   *Art at the Airports*, BAA Programme, Heathrow, Point
        West
1998   *Richard Hough Bursary*, Stills Gallery, Edinburgh
        Morning Star/Evening Star, Australian Centre for
        Contemporary Art catalogue to accompany the
        Melbourne – Scottish Cultural exchange
        From Here to There, High Street Projects, Christchurch,
        New Zealand
        Coil 7: Journal of the Moving Image
        This Island Earth, An Tuireann Gallery, Skye
1999   *Atopia 0.66*, Atopia Magazine
        Contemporary Sculpture in Scotland, Craftsman House,
        Australia
2001   *Here and Now*, Dundee Contemporary Arts

Acknowledgements

The artists would like to express their particular gratitude to Liz Skullina, Claire Scullion and Neil Symington, who have provided invaluable assistance, encouragement and opinions during the making of this book and many of the projects documented within it. Dalziel + Scullion would also like to thank the following individuals, without whom many of their works would not have been realised:

Judy Adam, Howie B, Alison Bain, Nicola Black, Rob Breen, Kevin and Sandra Bruce, Ruby Buchan, John Calcutt, Jane Catlin, Amanda Catto, Steve Chettle, Susan Christie, Pippa Coles, Amanda Crabtree, Alastair Downie, Bruno Dupont, Tom Eccles, Amanda Farr, Judith Findlay, Michael R. Forsythe, Doug Fowlie, Claire French, Stuart Frost, Ann Gallagher, Frank Gillingham, Jamie Goulding, Keith Hartley, Kenny Hunter, Stevie Hurrel, Iain Irving, Isaac Jackson, Geir Jenssen, Jim Johnston, Alison Kubler, Giles Lane, Clare Lilley, Phillip Long, Ian MacAuley, Claire MacDonald, Will Maclean, Helen McGill, Rachael May, Jennifer Melville, Kim Miller, Mandy Mitchell, Ciaran Monaghan, Tim Niel, Ian Nicoll, Andrew Patrizio, Julia Radcliffe, Alan Robb, Alistar Savage, Joe and Ailie Scullion, Julie Seddon Jones, Hector Smith, Gavin Sutherland, Simon Thorogood, Sally Townsend, Alasdair Wallace, David Ward, David Watson Hood, Cherry White, Nicola White, Claire Williams and Claudia Zeiske

And finally the staff of The Fruitmarket Gallery, in particular Siobhan Dougherty, George Gilliland, Lindsay Isaacs, Juliet Knight, Elizabeth McLean, Graeme Murray and the installation team.

Catalogue published to accompany *Home*, an exhibition of new work by Dalziel + Scullion commissioned by The Fruitmarket Gallery in collaboration with Milton Keynes Gallery and Manchester Art Gallery.

The Fruitmarket Gallery, Edinburgh
1 December 2001 to 12 January 2002

Milton Keynes Gallery
9 March to 28 April 2002

Manchester Art Gallery
7 December 2002 to 2 February 2003

Exhibition funded by The Henry Moore Foundation and the National Touring Programme through The Arts Council of England. Further funding was received for the publication from The Scottish Arts Council, PESCA and the Carnegie Trust for the Universities of Scotland. The new work was assisted by a Scottish Arts Council Visual Artists' Award.

Publication designed and typeset by Juliet Knight, Elizabeth McLean, Matthew Dalziel and Louise Scullion.

Photo credits:
John Carroll (*Bridgette, artists' dog*, p. 1)
Kevin McLean (*The Bathers*, p. 17)
Ruth Clark (*The Horn*, p. 33)
Stephen White (*Migrator*, pp. 37)
Antonia Reeve (*Endlessly*, p. 39)
Mike Davidson (*Modern Nature*, pp. 64-65)
Ruth Clark (*Sanctuary Furniture*, pp. 66-67)
Stephen White (*Meltwater*, pp. 68-69)
Jonty Wilde (*Voyager*, p. 70)
Alan Dimmick (*Home*, pp. 71-83)
Claire Scullion (artists with son, Ethan, p. 95)
All other photographs by Dalziel + Scullion

The Fruitmarket Gallery is indebted to a large number of people for their support, advice and practical assistance during the making of this exhibition and publication. We would particularly like to thank the following:

Amanda Catto, Judith Findlay, Keith Hartley, Natasha Howes, Clare Lilley, Timothy Llewellyn, Hilary Nicoll, Sue Pirnie, Stephen Snoddy, David Thorp, Emma Underhill, David Ward and Tim Wilcox.

Catalogue published by:
The Fruitmarket Gallery
45 Market Street
Edinburgh
EH1 1DF
Tel. +44 (0) 131 225 2383
Fax. +44 (0) 131 220 3130
www.fruitmarket.co.uk

The Fruitmarket Gallery is subsidised by The Scottish Arts Council
Scottish Charity No. SC 005576

Catalogue printed in an edition of 1,500 copies by Specialblue, London
Printed in the UK
ISBN 0 947912 08 8